WROCŁAW
THE MEETING PLACE

PHOTOGRAPHS
STANISŁAW KLIMEK
TEXT
BEATA MACIEJEWSKA

VIA NOVA

Edition of the Polish text by Marcin Grabski, Olga Rutkowska
Translated by Agnieszka Ziajka-Małecka

Wydawnictwo VIA NOVA
50-077 Wrocław, ul. Kazimierza Wielkiego 39, Poland
Phone: (0048 71) 344 23 77, Fax: (0048 71) 343 78 71
www.vianova.com.pl
ISBN 978-83-60544-42-6

WHERE EAST MEETS WEST

The Oder, by which thou layest
and by the restless current of which
Thou breakest into many streams,
That from their source to their estuary
Or flowing through all northern lands –
Findeth nowhere one to rival thee
O Wrocław [1]

– thus wrote Barthel (Bartholomäus) Stein, author of a 16th century description of the city of Wrocław. And since he was a man who travelled a lot – he studied in Krakow and Wien, worked in Wittenberg and Leipzig – his words are surely worthy of belief...

He was not the first person to be impressed by the city on the Oder. In a book written for the Sicilian King Roger the Arab, geographer al-Edrisi praised Wrocław as "a city famous for its scholars and craftsmen," and a Franciscan pilgrim Antonius went as far as saying that "Jerusalem is as big as Wrocław but not built as beautifully".

[1] Based on the translation from Latin by Marek Krajewski

3

The Main Square is the heart of Wrocław. It is here that people talk business and strengthen ties with their friends. It has been so for the last eight centuries, and Wrocław inhabitants treasure tradition. No wonder that the former Heimann's bank (33, Rynek), dating back to Napoleonic times, still houses a bank, and the Barasch brothers' department store (today "Feniks") has been a retail outlet for a hundred years.

The Wrocław Main Square is one of the biggest and most beautiful historical market squares in Europe. It was founded at the intersection of important transportation routes from the South – from Czech – to the North, and from Western Europe towards the East. From the very beginning of history international trade blossomed here and thanks to this the inhabitants of Wrocław became very wealthy, as did the city – huge sums (taxes) poured into the city coffers. In 15th century Wrocław more people traded here than in Prague, Ypres, Brno or Frankfurt am Main. And they did it very successfully. The square has never become an open air museum even though its historic buildings often date back to medieval times and are fairy-tale like. The inhabitants of Wrocław still meet here on business and for pleasure.

Illustration on page 3: Wrocław's coat of arms was granted to the city in 1530 by the Czech and Hungarian King Ferdinand I, and was later approved by Emperor Charles V. In the centre is the head of St. John the Baptist, patron saint of the city and the cathedral. In the top left-hand corner a rearing lion in a crown, the symbol of the Czech king, next to which is the Silesian eagle. Below is a bust of St. John the Evangelist on the upturned crown. The 'W' letter in Wrocław's coat of arms alludes to a legendary founder of the city named Wratislav (Wratysław). (The photograph shows the coat of arms of 1616 on the western façade of the City Hall.)

Wrocław's Main Square is one of the biggest in Europe and was delineated after the Mongol invasion of 1241. In the foreground, in the centre of the Square, is the New City Hall erected at the end of the 19th century, now the seat of Wrocław's Mayor and local authorities. In the photograph is the Main Square during the final concert of an annual national charity action called the Great Orchestra of Christmas Aid (12 January 2003).

Apart from the Main Square there are two more market squares in Wrocław – the New Market (Nowy Targ) and the Salt Market (plac Solny). Although they are located on different sides of the Old Town, we can see both from one point in Odrzańska Street (a side street leading off the Main Square) near Stare Jatki (a side street off Odrzańska Street); first we have to face east (to see the New Market), then south (the Salt Market).

The smallest of the market squares, vibrant with life since the Middle Ages, is the Salt Market. It derives its name from salt stalls that were located in the northern part of the square. People could also buy honey and wax here, precious furs, caviar, tea, and even goat's meat. The last salt stalls were removed in 1815 yet trade is still present in the square. Florists sell their goods till late at night. It is also a meeting place for lovers, who meet at the fountain with dragons or wait patiently under the stone spire.

As early as the Middle Ages, number 3 the Salt Market was one of the best known Wrocław pharmacies. Its coat of arms was a Negro. It is still standing on the façade and is worth looking at even though it is of modern origin. The black man, scantily dressed, is a bronze cast of the well-known Wrocław graphic artist Eugeniusz Get-Stankiewicz. The only difference between this monument and the original is the skin colour.

From the Main Square and the Salt Market branch streets of medieval origin: Odrzańska, Oławska and św. Mikołaja. However, they cannot compete with Świdnicka Street, which has the style and elegance of a great lady, though its beauty is slightly covered with dust of time. Times and people change but in Świdnicka Street you can still feel the pulse of the city.

In the Middle Ages the route from Pomerania and Wielkopolska to Silesia and Świdnica, ran through this street. These were the times when the street saw

A monument of Bolesław Chrobry (the Brave), the first king of Poland, crowned in 1025, was erected in Świdnicka Street in 2007. Although the ruler never visited Wrocław in person, it was thanks to him and emperor Otto III that the city became a seat of bishopric in the year 1000. Until World War II in this place was a monument of Wilhelm (William) I, king of Prussia, and since 1871 the emperor of united Germany.

many scoundrels of the darkest hue. They didn't come there freelyly but were led to the execution site. A procession of onlookers accompanying the convicts first passed by the internal Świdnicka Gate (located at the junction of Świdnicka Street with today Stanisława Leszczyńskiego Street), then passed by the Church of Sts. Stanislaus, Wenceslas, and Dorothy, and through the external Świdnicka Gate, near the Church of Corpus Christi, they then went outside the city walls. Here, in the Świdnickie Suburb, public executions were held since the 15th century – convicts prepared themselves for death in the small cemetery chapel of St. Gertrude, located next to the square, where later on a department store belonging to the Wertheim Company (now "Renoma") was erected.

The oldest and most monumental buildings in Świdnicka Street are two Gothic churches – of Corpus Christi and of Sts. Stanislaus, Wenceslas, and Dorothy. The legend has it that when Wrocław is to be afflicted by a disaster, the second church is vacated by a ghostly procession of armoured knights. They walk with their heads bent, barely touching the ground and hold burning torches in their hands. The last time they were seen was in the 17th century, when the plague was wreaking havoc in Wrocław. Instead of watching out for the ghostly procession, it is better to have a look at the... roof. It is the tallest Gothic roof in Poland. Its attic could house a seven-storey building.

From the end of the 18th century Świdnicka Street had become more and more elegant with magnificent shops and department stores, residences of members from the financial circles, art galleries and cafes. In the 1980s the street witnessed the famous happenings of the Orange Alternative movement which fought the communist system with laughter, exposing its absurdities. Świdnicka Street saw dwarves, secret KGB and CIA agents, and an army of Santa Clauses arrested by the militia. It is here that you could assess the rhetorical skills of future MPs of free Poland. Pacifists, militarists, revolutionary leftists and far-rightists, animal rights activists and human rights activists – all of them demonstrated their views here.

The birthplace of Wrocław is Ostrów Tumski (Cathedral Island). Here, at the beginning of the 10th century, near a crossing on the Oder, a town was erected for defensive purposes. Most probably it was the Czechs who erected it to strengthen the borders of their territory.

The first mention of Wrocław – from the year 1000 – was by Bishop Thietmar of Merseburg. In his description of the emperor Otto III's pilgrimage to

Images of St. John the Baptist can be seen on houses throughout Wrocław as well as on paving stones and public utility buildings. He is the patron saint of the cathedral and the city. The oldest representation of the saint dates back to around 1160. In the 15th century it was placed on the northern wall of the cathedral. Nowadays we may see a replica there. The original, damaged during the bombardment of the city by Russian aircraft at Easter 1945, is kept in the Archdiocesan Museum.

St. Adalbert's tomb (St. Vojtech) in Gniezno he mentions the creation of an ecclesiastical organization in the territory of Bolesław Chrobry (the Brave), Mieszko I's son. He describs Wrocław as a seat of one of the three bishoprics subordinate to the metropolis in Gniezno. He refers to the city as both Wrotizla and Wortizlava, however its current name comes from Wratysław; its Czech version was Vratislav and the Polish equivalent was Wrocisław, meaning "the one who is to come back famous." The history and legends don't feature the man who gave the city its name. Poles claim that he may have been a local tribal leader, Czechs believe him to have been Prince Vratislav.

However, one thing is certain – Wrocław achieved the fame promised by its name and the choice of the city as a seat of the bishopric shows how significant it was for the Piast monarchy. The chronicler Gall Anonim (the Anonymous Gaul) mentions the city as one of the few seats of the Kingdom of Poland – *sedes regni principales*. As early as the 11th century it was undoubtedly the capital of Silesia as it was where a deputy ruler, *comes provinciae,* resided.

Ostrów Tumski (the Cathedral Island) is Wrocław's *terra sancta*. In order to get there, one has to cross the Tumski Bridge, which was the border beyond which

The Tumski Bridge, connecting the Cathedral Island with Sand Island, was at the end of the 12th century the western border of the church jurisdiction, independent of the city. The current steel bridge was built in the years 1888–1889. In 1893 at the entrance to the bridge from the side of Sand Island two stone monuments were located, monuments of patron saints of Silesia and the Wrocław diocese: St. Jadwiga (St. Hedwig) and St. John the Baptist.

the church jurisdiction started. Representatives of the lay authority, including princes, had to take off their headgear once they crossed the bridge.

Straight from the bridge one enters Katedralna Street, the most magical of the many magical streets in Wrocław. It is at its most beautiful at night. It was a Wrocław bishop himself who supervised development of this street, and erecting unpermitted buildings was severely punished. When in 1375 the Świętokrzyska Chapter was trying to build a row of outbuildings, among them a bakery and the fence closing Katedralna Street near the Collegiate Church of the Holy Cross, it was twice anathemized by the bishop. However, there were people who were not afraid of their shepherd's wrath and erected houses

Motifs of the Annunciation, a Silesian eagle as well as a Bohemian lion adorn the steel-padded doors, dating from about 1400, placed between the Council Chamber and the Council Office of the City Hall.

outside the pre-determined line of building development; that is why the street was narrowed by a third of its width, (planned at the end of the 13th century and beginning of the 14th century) and hence it obtained its slightly curved shape.

Monumental churches, the magnificent Gothic cathedral, houses of canons and the archbishop's palace are located there. When gas lamps and special floodlights light up at dusk bringing out the most beautiful architectural elements, Ostrów Tumski looks like a fairyland.

It is no wonder Wrocław has been so desirable since the beginning of its existence. It changed hands. It belonged to Czechs, Poles, Hungarians, Austrians and Germans. Walloons, Jews, Italians, Ruthenians settled here; nations, religions and cultures mixed with one another. The first reference to Wrocław dates back to the year 1000 when the city on the Oder became a seat of bishopric. Then it was within the territory of the Piast state and it changed in 1335, when it became part of the Czech Crown. It was a rich, populous, well-developed city, second in terms of importance after Prague. Royal privileges were showered upon Wrocław in abundance, international trade was blossomed and culture was developed.

Transition under the Habsburg rule in 1526 started a political collapse of the city. A ban on appeal to courts in Magdeburg was issued, and the Royal Chamber to manage fiscal issues of the city and Silesia was set up.

Wrocław experienced disastrous destruction caused by the Thirty Years War and epidemics ravaging the population. But it obtained the Leopoldine Academy (today the University of Wrocław), splendid Baroque churches and palaces.

Wrocław was taken away from the Habsburgs by the Prussian King Frederick the Great, who in 1741 committed "the most sensational crime of modern times" and, taking advantage of Austria's weakness, occupied Silesia. For the Silesian Protestants he wore the mantel of liberator from the slavery of the Catholic Habsburgs. And even though the enthusiasm of inhabitants subsided as soon as the king reached into their pockets, the city remained part of the Prussian state until 1870, when it became part of the German Reich. This was the time of economic and urban planning development of the city. The process was hampered by World War I, economic crises, political terror under the Third Reich, nevertheless the city transformed.

In the former palace of Prussian kings (now the seat of the Municipal Museum in Kazimierza Wielkiego Street) King Frederick William III established in 1813 the highest German wartime order, the Iron Cross, and signed the famous manifesto "An mein Volk" ("To my nation"), a call to arms against Napoleon.

After *Festung Breslau* Wrocław was entirely ruined. 21,600 houses out of 30,000 had been destroyed. In the photograph today's Powstańców Śląskich Street (Strasse der SA, before 1938 – Kaiser-Wilhelm-Strasse) in 1945. (Phot. Krystyna Gorazdowska, property of the Municipal Museum in Wrocław).

Silesia – called "the land of bridges" and "the meeting place" together with its capital has always been located "between", which is a great advantage to Wrocław, thanks to this it became a gate connecting the East and the West.

At the same time it is the place where, as in a lens of a microscope, you can see the history of Central Europe and understand the tragedies of the 20th century: Nazism, infinite destruction of World War II, extermination of European Jews, changing borders, forced resettlement and the division of the continent by the Iron Curtain. Wrocław witnessed two totalitarianisms – fascism and communism, in both Nazi and Stalinist versions.

The city experienced total destruction in 1945 at the time of the Festung Breslau defence and it became part of another state. The German Breslau became Polish Wrocław, and the borders of Poland were delineated by "the Big Three." At the conference in Potsdam Joseph Stalin enforced a concept of the western border of Poland on the Oder and Neisse – German territories east of both rivers were handed over by the allied forces to the Polish administration and the German population was to be resettled. For Breslauers it was expulsion.

New inhabitants came from the whole of Poland. Some had to settle here because, after the change of Poland's borders in the east, they had to leave their

The *Panorama Racławicka*, a work of Jan Styka and Wojciech Kossak, was exhibited in Lvov from 1894. The big painting represents the victorious first battle of the Kościuszko Insurrection. On the 4th April 1794 Polish troops defeated the Russian army at Racławice. Although the painting arrived in Wrocław in 1946 it was not displayed to the public until 1983 due to concern about the anti-Russian sentiments it might evoke.

In 2000, eleven years after the beginning of political transformation and the recovery of independence (the last Soviet troops left Poland in 1993), the city joyfully celebrated its millennium i.e. the thousandth anniversary of the first written record of Wroclaw and the creation of a bishopric here. On 24th of June (St. John the Baptist's Day) a patriotic mass was celebrated in the Main Square to commemorate the bishopric and the city.

homes. Ironically, they were called 'repatriants' even though they were chased out of their homeland and had to come to a foreign land. The eastern part of Poland, where they had been living for generations, became part of the Soviet Union. They brought their customs with them, a monument of Aleksander Fredro, the Polish poet, and treasures of the Ossolineum Institute. In this devastated city, so strange to them, they had to build a new life for themselves and their children. They proved their adventurous spirit, resourcefulness and openness. The inhabitants of Wrocław know the value of tolerance and respect for others. Because it is the meeting place.

Beata Maciejewska

1. "I must say a few words about the City Hall which is, indeed, most admirably beautiful" wrote a 19th century Polish writer Józef Ignacy Kraszewski. In the picture: the eastern façade in late-Gothic style (end of the 15th century). In front of the City Hall is the pillory which has recently been renovated.

2. The astronomical clock was placed on the eastern façade in 1580. The hand of the sun sphere indicates hours whereas the hand of the moon sphere – moon phases. At the corners are ancient Egyptian symbols for the seasons.

3–4. Heinrich von Korn, Wrocław's publisher, collector and art patron, was portrayed in the sculpture of a burger which was mounted on the southern façade of the City Hall in 1891. His figure became part of "The Gallery of Townspeople". Alexander Kaumann, a construction adviser in the 19th century Wrocław was portrayed in the costume of … a medieval Alderman.

5. Fragments of the frieze in the southern façade date back to the 15th century. In the photograph: a vender being wheeled in a barrel.

6. Late Gothic carved ornaments on the southern façade of the City Hall excellently correspond to the 19th century "Gallery of Townspeople" i.e. a gallery of several statues under canopies. The figures were conceived by Karl Lüdecke who also supervised their construction.

7. The oriel in the western façade of the City Hall which dates from 1504.

8. The western façade of the City Hall adorned with a tower with a Renaissance cupola. In front of the City Hall, the monument of count Aleksander Fredro, the Polish writer of comedies, which stood in Lvov from 1897 to the end of the Second World War. At present one of the most popular monuments in Wrocław.

9. The interiors of an old chapel on the first floor with a vault supported by one pillar. Currently it houses museum and occasionally functions as a small-audience concert hall. On the right is the portal over the entrance to the Grand Hall, on the left, the portal over the entrance to the old Chamber of the City Council Senior.

10. The Grand Hall of the City Hall, the middle nave. The portal which dates from about 1485 is adorned with coats of arms featuring the Czech lion, Silesian eagle and the bust of John the Evangelist, patron saint of the chapel in the City Hall. It is also evidence of Wrocław's dependence on the Czech Crown.

24

11–12. The middle oriel of the Grand Hall is decorated with sculpture dating from the turn of the 15th century. The entrance is marked symmetrically with figures of knights and monkeys.

13. The western part of the Main Square was already known as the Wool Market in the Middle Ages, and wool continued to be traded here until 1905 and few people were surprised by the presence of heaps of sacks. The western frontage of the Main Square is marked on the left with a "tower block" which was finished in 1931 as the former Municipal Savings Bank (currently Zachodni WBK Bank)

14. The Merchant's House formerly belonging to the brothers Arthur and George Barasch (today's "Feniks" department store) is built into the eastern frontage of the Main Square. The art nouveau building was crowned with a lit crystal globe with the diameter of 6.5 m which was destroyed in 1929 by lightning.

15. The Glass Fountain, built in the western part of the Main Square to the design of the Wrocław sculptor Alojzy Gryt is called "Zdrój" (the spring) after the name of the former Mayor of Wrocław (1990–2001), Bogdan Zdrojewski. He was an ardent advocate of the controversial form of the fountain.

16. The southwestern part of the Main Square with the monument to Aleksander Fredro in the foreground. The area is a popular meeting point for courting couples and the site of political demonstrations.

17. The historic houses, nowadays called Jaś i Małgosia (Hensel and Gretchen) were formerly the homes of altar service members of the adjacent St. Elisabeth's Church. Jaś (the smaller one) dates from the Renaissance period, whereas Małgosia dates from the Baroque.

18. St. Elisabeth's Church (which holds the title of basilica) has functioned as a parish church since 1245. In 1999 a monument (by Karl Biedermann) was erected in the square adjacent to the church. The monument commemorates Dietrich Bonhoeffer, an inhabitant of Wrocław, born in 1906, and Protestant theologian who was involved in an ecumenical and anti-Nazi movement. He was executed in the Flossenburg concentration camp in 1945.

19. St. Elisabeth's Church, apart from fulfilling religious functions (Roman Catholic military and civil parish church), is also the venue for concerts.

20. St. Elisabeth's Church had strong historical ties with Poland, especially in the 16th and 17th centuries. Its clergymen were known for their merits for the presence of the Polish language in Evangelical services in Silesia (Jan Akolut, among others).

21. St. Elisabeth's Church is a mausoleum for the most affluent burgher families of Wrocław. Many of the people buried here chose to live in Wrocław having arrived in the city from Saxony, Bavaria, Hungary and Poland. The main element of the epitaph (from 1585) of Nicklas Rehdiger, patrician and city councillor, are figures of his family members, men and women, kneeling opposite each other (in the photograph: close-up).

22. The tomb monument of Johann Georg von Wolff (from 1722), the Emperor's adviser and senator, was executed according to a design by Joseph Emmanuel Fischer von Erlach. The sculpture composition (7.5 m high) is deeply symbolic.

23. The mannerist tombstone, erected by the patrician Heinrich Rybisch (to commemorate himself) in St. Elisabeth's Church, was considered a manifestation of pride in the 16th century Wrocław, the inhabitants of which smeared it with axel grease.

24. The view from the tower of St. Elisabeth's Church overlooking Ostrów Tumski (Tumski Island) and Wyspa Piaskowa (Sand Island). On the right, in the background is the cathedral. On the left: the dark silhouette of the Church of Our Lady. In the background can be seen the tower and Church of the Holy Cross.

25. The view from the tower of St. Elisabeth's Church towards the West i.e. the former Mikołajskie Suburbs incorporated into the city after the demolition of its fortifications in 1807 at the command of Jerôme Bonaparte, brother of Napoleon.

40

26. The present-day Kiełbaśnicza Street dates back to the foundation lay-out of 1242. On the corner of today's Łazienna Street is the Gothic and Renaissance historic building of George Baumann's printing-house where, starting from 1632, the first newspaper of Wrocław was printed.

27. The present-day Jatki, the passage existing already in 1266, was then famous for its butchers' stands. In the course of time butchers were replaced by artists. Today only bronze monuments of animals serve as a reminder of the street's past.

28. The Old Exchange in the Salt Market was erected between 1822 and 1825. Architect Karl Ferdinand Langhans gave the exchange the character of an Italian municipal palace of the Renaissance period.

29. In the Salt Market dating from the time when the Main Square was delineated, not only salt was sold here but also honey, leather, ropes and goat's meat. The square was also called the Polish Square due to the fact that many of the merchants there were Polish.

30. The view from the Main Square overlooking the Salt Market. The southern side of the Main Square was called the side of Golden Cup (named after the emblem of one of the historic houses).

31. The Church of St. Mary Magdalene was the second parish church of the medieval city (the Church of St. Elisabeth being the first one).

32. The tombstone of the syndic and imperial adviser Caspar Artzat (dated from 1679) is located in the Church of St. Mary Magdalene and was made by the Tyrolian artist Mathias Rauchmiller who was active at the Emperor's court in Vienna.

33. The Sacrament-house of the church of St. Mary Magdalene dating back to the end of the 14th century shows scenes of Christ's Passion: Flogging, Crucifixion and Resurrection (in the photograph).

34. The Romanesque portal (12th century) originating from the Benedictine Abbey (taken to pieces in 1529) in Ołbin (German Elbing) was built in the external walls of St. Mary Magdalene's Church in 1546.

35. It was in Świdnicka Street, which used to be the most important and elegant street in the city, that in 1841, a building of the Municipal Theatre was erected (now the Opera of Wrocław). In the background we can see the "Monopol" hotel and the church of Sts. Stanislaus, Wenceslas and Dorothy.

36. The building, designed by Karl Ferdinand Langhans in 1837, was rebuilt twice after fires. The most recent renovation was completed in 2007.

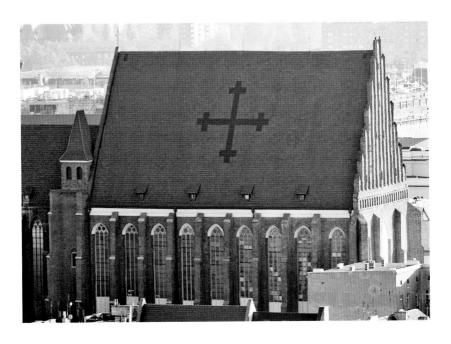

37. The shrine of three nations under the protection of St. Stanislaus, the patron saint of Poland, St. Wenceslas, the patron saint of the Czech Crown and St. Dorothy, the patron saint of German settlers. The church was founded in 1351 by Emperor Charles IV during his visit to Wrocław.

38. Baron Heinrich Gottfried von Spaetgen was a secretary at the court of Emperor Charles VI. His tombstone in St. Dorothy's Church, executed by Franz Joseph Mangoldt, reflects the social status of the baron. The photograph shows a close-up of a symbolic figure on the tombstone: Chronos, personification of time and eternity.

52

39. Here in 1267 there was a cemetery chapel of Mary of Egypt, belonging to the parish of St. Mary Magdalene. The church was erected in its present form at the beginning of the 15th century, and was soon dedicated to St. Christopher. Between 1416–1829 Polish sermons were delivered here and a Polish school functioned at the church. Presently this Evangelical Church is the seat of a German-speaking Parish.

40. The Church of St. Christopher was enlarged in the Renaissance period. In the photograph: a close-up of the tombstone built into the northern wall of the church.

41–42. The Boulevard on Sand Island, surrounding the Church of Our Lady and the building of a former monastery of Canons Regular, is named after Piotr Włostowic (Peter Wlast), the founder of the original church and monastery of the 12th century.

Across the Odra River is the panorama of Tumski Island with the towers of the Cathedral of St. John the Baptist (on the right) and the Church of the Holy Cross (on the left).

43. "From the other bank, I shall remember the light of lanterns. / A splendid sight reflected on the river" – wrote the German theologian Joachim Konrad in a poem about Tumski Island.

44. A view from Kapitulna Street overlooking the Cathedral of St. John the Baptist; the baroque chapel of Resurrection in the background.

45. The Tumski Bridge (*Pons Cathedralis*) leading from Sand Island to Tumski Island once formed a border beyond which ecclesiastical jurisdiction was in force. From 1504 up to 1810 the municipal court could not prosecute criminals who crossed the bridge.

46. In Gothic and Renaissance building of the Chapter (beginning of the 16th century), in the vicinity of the Cathedral, the archives and library of the diocese were kept to the end of the 19th century. Currently the building forms part of the Archdiocesan Museum.

47. The Arcade which joins the Church of St. Giles on Tumski Island (the oldest preserved church in Wrocław) with the building of the Chapter (on the left) is called the noodle gate. According to the legend, the stone noodle on the arcade is the trace of a great love – here the ghost of a wife fed her husband delicious Silesian noodles.

48. St. Mary's statue in front of St. John the Baptist's Cathedral stood there in 1694 on the Cathedral Chapter's initiative.

49. The Cathedral's 15th century western portico was rebuilt in the 19th century. However, many elements of the old decorations were preserved. In the niches: stone statues of St. Gregory the Great and St. Paul.

50. The figure of St. Jadwiga (St. Hedwig) of the cathedral's western portico. This saint came from Andechs in Bavaria and was a wife of Henry the Bearded, Piast Duke of Silesia. In her left hand she holds the miniature of the Cistercian church in Trzebnica (she was its founder), in her right hand – the figure of the Holy Virgin she never parted with.

51. A view of the Cathedral from the East. The two baroque chapels: St. Elisabeth's (on the left) and Electoral (on the right) are accompanied by the Gothic chapel of St. Mary (in the middle). The neo-Gothic towers are surmounted by cupolas built as late as 1991 (the old ones having been destroyed during the War) and mounted by means of a helicopter.

52. The cathedral's crypt exhibits the stone relics (dated from the 10th – 12th centuries) of the earlier buildings which stood in that place. The present-day shrine was constructed in stages from the 13th century onwards.

53. The Cathedral's nave and presbytery dating from the 13th century are shown in the background. During the *Festung Breslau* siege, the Cathedral was so badly damaged that many doubted whether reconstruction would be possible.

54–55. St. Elisabeth's Chapel (from Thuringia) in the cathedral was founded between 1680–1700 by Friedrich von Hessen, Landgrave of Hesse (bishop of Wrocław from 1671) who was eventually buried here. His tombstone (both a close-up and a general view of which are shown in the photographs) was made by Domenico Guidi.

56. A view from the Cathedral's tower. On the right stands the Church of the Holy Cross, in the middle, Sand Island with the Church of Our Lady and the former monastery of Canons Regular (currently the University Library).

57. A view from the tower of the Church of the Holy Cross overlooking the cathedral. The oldest part of the city was situated here, on Tumski Island. Most probably it was built by the Czech at the beginning of the 10th century.

58. St. Martin's Church, the chapel of the medieval city on Tumski Island. It was built in the 13th century and has changed little since. In the background stands the Church of the Holy Cross.

59. The Church of the Holy Cross was founded in 1288 by Duke Henry IV the Righteous to celebrate his reconciliation with bishop Tomasz II (Thomas II) and was intended to be the necropolis of Wrocław's Piasts. It has a reputation for being the most beautiful Gothic church in Wrocław.

60–61. The Botanical Gardens were established during the period 1811–16, as a university institution. The Gardens house the University Museum of Natural History (formerly the Zoological Museum).

62. "It is due to the Jesuits that we have that old and beautiful building of thick walls and of deep window niches with the richly ornamented baroque »Aula Leopoldina« and the »Concert Hall«" wrote Edith Stein, the later patron saint of Europe, about the university in 1911. In the photograph, the university building, the view from the tower of St. Elisabeth's Church.

63. Jesuit Leopold University of Wrocław was established due to the donation of the castle by the Odra River to the Jesuits by Emperor Leopold I. The University opened in 1702 and a new baroque building was erected in the years 1728–1743.

64–65. Four allegorical figures, symbols of the four university faculties, were put on the balcony balustrade of the Mathematics Tower of the University in 1733. Theology and Law are shown in the photographs.

66. The main university entrance is decorated with a balcony portico with allegorical statues symbolising The Four Cardinal Virtues. Justice wields a sword.

67. University Concert Hall, formerly the *Oratorium Marianum*, was destroyed in 1945. As late as 1997 it was reopened to public after reconstruction which was made possible due to the photographic records from 1944 preserved in the Herder Institute in Marburg.

68–69. Aula Leopoldina, a splendid baroque hall where the architecture, painting and sculpture form a homogenous unity. Over the podium stands the apotheosis of Emperor Leopold II, the founder of the University. The figures of a bearded thinker with an ardent heart (in the photograph) and a woman with a beehive (representing Discernment and Diligence) accompany Leopold personifying the Emperor's motto *Consilio et Industria*.

70–71. The Jesuit Church of the Holy Name of Jesus is one of the most beautiful baroque interiors in Silesia. The magnificent paintings were created by Johann Michael Rottmayer, the founder of the Austrian Baroque Painting School. The church's dynamic and sculpture interior decorations were the result of a thorough reconstruction carried out from 1722 onward by the extraordinary architect and artist Jesuit Christophorus Tausch.

72–73. The former monastery of Crusaders with a Red Star was one of the biggest baroque projects in Wrocław. In 1810 the Catholic St. Matthias Gymnasium was based here. After the Second World War the monastery became the seat of the Zakład

Narodowy im. Ossolińskich (the Ossolineum Institute), moved here from Lvov, which houses many treasures of Polish culture. In the courtyard, regarded as a "magical place", stands a beautiful baroque well.

74–75. The building of the former Province Management was finished in 1886. Currently it houses the National Museum (former Silesian Museum) with the saved collections of two other city museums which were destroyed during the Second World War: The

Silesian Museum of Artistic Handicraft and Ancient Times and The Silesian Museum of Fine Arts. It also houses a collection of Polish art (from 17th to 19th centuries) originating from Lvov and Vilnius as well as Poland's biggest collection of Polish modern art.

76. Jaxa's (Peter Wlast's son-in-law) foundation tympanum from the monastery Church of St. Michael Archangel in Ołbin dated back to 1150–1163. Ołbin was in the 12th century the most densely inhabited district in the city and within the abbey there were as many as 3 churches. The tympanum and other relics of Romanesque art are currently exhibited in the Architecture Museum (in today's Bernardyńska Street).

77. A cloister garth in a museum? Yes. The Architecture Museum is based in the post-Bernardine Monastery, therefore it has its cloister garth. The monastery buildings, erected in the 15th and 16th centuries, were largely destroyed in 1945. Reconstruction was carried out according to a design of Edward Małachowicz from 1956 to 1974.

78. The Mikołajski Arsenal (in the present-day Antoni Cieszyński Street) shows that Wrocław was once a fortress. In the past, food and arms were stored here. Today it plays home to the museum exhibits and archival materials that are stored here.

79. St. Adalbert's Church originally served the first municipal parish. It is situated by the primaeval route North-South, leading through a historical crossing of the Odra River (through Sand Island). In the photograph is shown a close-up of the 13th century frieze on the southern façade.

80. In 1226 St. Adalbert's Church was taken over by the Dominicans who arrived from Kraków under the leadership of Czesław Odrowąż. The baroque chapel, erected over the period 1711–1730, houses the alabaster sarcophagus of the blessed Czesław.

81. The baroque Church of the Holy Trinity (Traugutta Street), with perfectly preserved interiors, belongs to the Brothers of St. John of God order (Bonifratrzy), who arrived in Wrocław in 1711. Traditionally they have specialized in phytotherapy.

82–83. The Church of God's Providence was raised between 1746 and 1759 as the court church on the initiative of Frederick II, the King of Prussia. Nowadays it is the main shrine of the Evangelical-Lutheran Church in the diocese of Wrocław. It is one of four churches (next to the Synagogue, Orthodox Church and the Catholic Church of St. Nicolas) situated in the neighbourhood as part of the so-designated District of Mutual Respect.

84. Fortunately, the White Stork Synagogue was not damaged by the Nazis. It is an outstanding example of Classicism designed by Karl Ferdinand Langhans. The Jewish community, once numerous and affluent, was exterminated during the Second World War. Now, the synagogue is owned by the present small Jewish community. It is one of the four shrines in the District of Mutual Respect.

85. The cemetery chapel of St. Elisabeth's parish was erected here (today's Św. Mikołaja Street) at the end of 13th century. St. Barbara's Church took its Gothic shape at the end of the 15th century. Since 1963 it has been an Orthodox church which cooperates with churches of other denominations in the District of Mutual Respect. In the photograph is the iconostasis in the sacristy of the church.

86. St. Maurice's Church (today's Traugutta Street), mentioned in the records as early as 1234, was surrounded by a Valon settlement in the Middle Ages. The last German parish priest of St. Maurice's parish, Reverend Paul Peikert was the author of a terryfying chronicle of the *Festung Breslau* siege.

87. The classicistic epitaph of the Fryderyk Jakub and Ksawery Psarski's was built in the southern wall of St. Maurice's Church in 1806.

88–89. The University Library (today's Szajnochy Street) is housed in the 19th century building of a former Municipal Library. Before the Second World War the whole library collection was located in a former monastery building on Sand Island (at present only the special collection of the library is kept there). During the War the most precious part of the collection was evacuated. The volumes which remained in Wrocław (approx. 500,000) were burnt on the night of 9th May 1945. Apart from the general collection, the library possesses a unique collection of manuscripts, old prints, graphic and cartographic collection connected with the history of Silesia.

90. The palace erected in the years 1785–87 (Szajnochy Street) for Gideon von Pachaly, the main tax collector in the War and Domain Chamber, designed by Karl Gotthard Langhans. The building now belongs to the University Library.

91. The building of the former municipal baths (today's Skłodowskiej-Curie Street) constructed according to a design by Max Berg during the period 1912–1914. Apart from the baths, it also housed the Revenue Office and a shelter for single mothers.

92. In the water-tower in the present-day Na Grobli Street one can see the unique 18-metre high steel construction of a pumping-steam machine dating from 1879. Nowadays the water-tower building functions as a museum and a stage for theatrical performances.

93. The wooden Przedtumski Bridge was a part of a historical crossing of the Odra River. In 1885 a steel construction called the Gneisenau Bridge was erected there. Today the bridge is called "Młyński" (The Mill Bridge) and connects St. Jadwiga Street with the present-day Bema Square.

94. The 19th century Zwierzyniecki Bridge (formerly "Passbrücke"), located in the western part of the city, is supported by four columns of red sandstone. It is adorned with low reliefs featuring motifs from Wrocław's coat of arms.

95. Wrocław's most famous bridge, has been called the Grunwaldzki Bridge since 1947 (before the War it was known as the Emperor's Bridge). It used to be the second largest suspension bridge in Germany.

96. The former department store at today's 32 Rzeźnicza Street was opened in 1901. The building belonged to the Schlesinger & Grünbaum company which dealt in the wholesale of ready-made clothing for men and boys. The company ceased to operate due to persecution of Jews before 1939.

97. The decision to build the Royal Higher Technical School was taken in 1902. The block of school buildings (today the Technical University of Wrocław) was erected in a few stages from 1905 onwards. In the photograph is the entrance (Norwida Street) to the main building, built in the first stage of construction.

98. The present-day main building of the Technical University of Wrocław in Wybrzeże Wyspiańskiego Street was erected as late as 1925–1928. It was designed by Max Schrimer and Heinrich Müller.

99. The machine laboratory of the Royal Higher Technical School (in the present-day Smoluchowskiego Street) was created in the first stage of the construction of the block between 1905–1910.

100–101. The Centennial Hall, situated in the vicinity of the Szczytnicki Park, in the eastern part of the city, was erected in 1913 to celebrate a hundredth anniversary of the war to liberate Prussia from Napoleon's army. The investment was financed from the municipal coffers, some councilors protested, saying that the money should not be wasted on a building resembling "a gas container" or "a hat-box".

102. The Hall, presently called the People's Hall, is a work of Max Berg, the eminent architect. Enthusiasts compared in to Babylonian ziggurats and the Hagia Sophia church in Constantinopolis. A water pool surrounded by a pergola (designed by Hans Poelzig) is located next to the Hall, on the side of the Szczytnicki Park.

103. The building was one of the first buildings created for the so-called "mass recipient." The Hall is the place of theatrical performances, musical concerts (once the Hall housed the biggest organs in the city), pre-election meetings, sporting events, religious gatherings (in 1997 the pope John Paul II prayed here) and even opera stagings.

104. At the time of opening in 1913 the Centennial Hall was admired as the biggest ferro-concrete construction in the world. The dimensions of the Hall are also impressive – the diameter of the dome amounts to 65 m (over 20 m more than the Roman Pantheon) and the height – to 42 m.

105. The former exhibition pavilion, so called Pavilion of Four Domes (designed by Hans Poelzig), the seat of the Historical Exhibition of 1913. In 1952 it became the seat of the Feature Film Company. The first film – a crime story – was shot a year later.

106. The bird's-eye view shows the Hall and the Pavilion of Four Domes (on the left). Iglica (the needle-shaped construction) designed by Stanisław Hempel, situated in front of the Hall, has remained there after the Exhibition of Recovered Territory (held in 1948).

107. The 16th century Church of St. John Nepomuk has been located in the Szczytnicki Park since 1913. Together with a rural cemetery it was one of the exhibitions on the Exhibition of Cemetery Art, accompanying the Century Exhibition.

108. The Szczytnicki Park (named after an old village of Alt-Schietnig) became a municipal property as late as in the second half of the 19th century. Beforehand, at the end of the 18th century, the English-style park was created here by the duke Friedrich Ludwig von Hohenlohe-Ingelfingen who made it available to inhabitants of Wrocław as the first open park in the city.

109. This house attracts architects from all over the world. It was designed by Hans Scharoun for single people and childless couples. Enthusiasts wrote that it looked like a ship anchored in port. This exemplary building (in today's Kopernika Street, in the vicinity of the Szczytnicki Park) was an element of the WuWA "Wohnung und Werkraum" (Flat and Workplace) exhibition of 1929.

110. The first modern department store in Wrocław (former Petersdorff, presently "Kameleon" department store in the present-day Szewska Street) erected in 1929 to an expressive design of Erich Mendelsohn. Even today it is admired for the elegance of its avant-guard shape. It reminds us that it is trade that has always made Wrocław go round.

111. The housing estate of semi-detached houses in Ołtaszyn (in today's Strączkowa Street), designed by Ernst May, built between 1921 and 1922 for farm workers. A modern, yet modest social scheme was combined here with a kind of rural house surrounded by a garden.

112. The main square of the Karłowice housing estate embodying the idea of a city-garden. It became part of Wrocław as late as in 1928 as a luxurious villa district.

113. Tadeusz Kościuszko Square (formerly the square of Prussian general Friedrich Bogislav von Tauentzien). His monument, located in the centre of the square till 1945, was placed there in 1795, where the square itself did not exist. It was delineated in 1807, after pulling down the fortifications. Only few buildings in the square remained after the Second World War, including the building on the left, the biggest department store in the city, from 1928 the property of the Wertheim company (nowadays "Renoma" department store)

114. A bird's-eye view, on the left is an axel of the Bridge of Peace, on the right is an axel of the Grunwaldzki Bridge and Grunwaldzki Square, created as a result of planned burning and demolition of a compact development to build an airport (the action started on 7 March 1945). It is estimated that during this action, carried out at the time of Soviet bombardment, several thousand people lost their lives. These were prisoners of war and forced labourers of different nations (Poles included) as well as Wrocław's civilians.

115. The Southern Park was created in the years 1891–1892 thanks to the initiative of Julius Schottländer, the owner of parts of Borek and Partynice, southern districts of the city. In return for including them into a municipal gas network, Schottländer offered 20 ha to the city (between present-day Ślężna Street and Powstańców Śląskich Street) to be used as a municipal park.

116. The Jewish cemetery in Ślężna Street, nowadays a section of the Municipal Museum, is the only preserved 19th century cemetery in Wrocław. The first funeral took place on 17 November 1856 and the cemetery started to take the present-day form at the end of the 19th century.

134

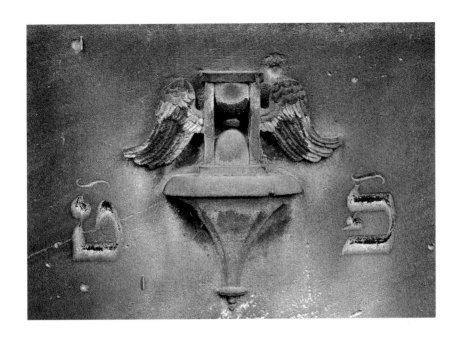

117–118. Tombstones, tomb monuments and tombs of the Jewish cemetery were created in various periods (also tomb plates, which are older than the cemetery itself and which were found in the city area, are exhibited here), hence the variety of styles and tastes. But they incorporate many common symbols e.g. hands in gesture of blessing symbolise a descendant of a high-priest, whereas an hourglass with winds denotes passing time.

119. The Cemetery of Russian Army Officers (in Karkonoska Avenue), who lost their lives during the siege of the city in 1945, has the shape designed for it by Tadeusz Ptaszycki in 1947. The monument of the soldiers, a monumental gloriette, was designed by Roman Feliński, first working in Lvov and then in Warsaw.

120. This tomb monument (1903) of high artistic value is one of the few old monuments preserved in the Grabiszyński cemetery.

121–122. In recent years the number of Wrocław's students increased twofold (to almost 130,000). The photograph shows new buildings of the Law, Administration and Economy Faculty at the University of Wrocław, in Kuźnicza Street (designed by Zbigniew Maćków and the team) and in Więzienna Street (designed by Ewa Frankiewicz).

123. The change of a political and economic system in 1989 brought about, among others, fast economic development. Today Wrocław is the seat of many Polish and foreign companies. The office building, built by the European Leasing Fund, was erected in Podwale Street, next to the former city moat (designed by Dorota Jarodzka--Śródka, Kazimierz Śródka).

124. "Wratislavia Center" is an architectural complex providing space for hotels, offices and commercial facilities (it was designed by Leszek Łękawa, Jerzy Chmura, Marek Krupiński). The building was erected in the vicinity of St. Elisabeth's Church, on the plot surrounded by historical streets: Kiełbaśnicza, św. Mikołaja and Rzeźnicza.

125. The building called "Silver Forum" in Strzegomska Street (designed by Dorota Jarodzka-Śródka and Kazimierz Śródka) is one of many office buildings being currently constructed in Wrocław. Annually about 6,000 new companies start up their business in the city (data from 2002).

126. Newly erected Wrocław hotels host foreign tourists visiting the city (about a million a year) as well as visitors coming to the capital city of the Lower Silesia on business. In the photograph is the "Park Plaza" hotel in Bolesława Drobnera Street (designed by Edward Lach with the team).

Index